EXTREME ANIMALS

Contents

Life at the extreme   2
Feeling the heat   4
The hottest place on Earth   6
Deadly dry   8
Chilling out   10
Feeling the freeze   12
Dizzy heights   14
Flying high   16
Down in the depths   18
At the bottom of the ocean   20
Poisonous places   22
Extreme defences   24
Nature's survivors   26
Glossary   28
Index   29
Adapting to extreme places   30

Written by Charlotte Guillain

Collins

Life at the extreme

All animals live in **habitats** that give them food, water and shelter. Animals' bodies have **adapted** over thousands of years to help them live in their particular habitat.

FACT >>>
Polar bears have thick layers of fat and fur to keep them warm.

Some animals live in the most extreme places on the planet. They have adapted in amazing ways to survive extreme heat or cold. Others live in very dry or poisonous places. These are nature's survivors, living life at the extreme.

FACT >>>
Camels can live for weeks without drinking water.

Feeling the heat

Deserts are the hottest places on Earth. Temperatures can become so high that most animals would die within minutes.

In the Sahara Desert, midday temperatures can reach over 50°C. Most animals living there hide underground at the hottest time of day. But Saharan silver ants come out of their nest to look for food. They feed on the bodies of animals that have died in the heat. How do the ants survive?

The ants can keep track of the sun's position to find their way back to their nests quickly.

Tough, silvery skin reflects the sunlight.

Long legs keep their bodies away from hot sand, and they can move very fast.

Special chemicals are produced in their bodies that help them to work in the extreme heat.

The hottest place on Earth

Death Valley in the United States is one of the hottest places on Earth. Few animals can survive there. But fringe-toed lizards have adapted to live on the baking sand of the valley floor.

FACT >>>
The lizards run on their back legs to get to top speed – four metres per second!

Scaly fringes on their back toes grip dry, loose sand when the lizards run across the hot desert.

The spade-shaped heads of fringe-toed lizards help them to burrow under sand to cool down and hide from **predators**.

Flaps over the lizards' ears and in their nostrils protect them from sand.

The lizards don't drink water. They get all the water they need from food.

Deadly dry

Most animals need to drink water often. But some animals can live for a long time with very little water.

The central desert of Australia is extremely dry. Sometimes there is no rain for years. Australian spadefoot toads survive in this wilderness by burying themselves underground during times of drought, sometimes for years at a time.

> The toads store water in their bodies to use while they're underground.

The toads only dig their way out of the sand when it finally rains.

Large front feet help the toads to dig underground holes to sleep in.

FACT >>>
Spadefoot toads spend most of their time asleep underground.

Chilling out

At the other extreme, many animals survive in below-freezing temperatures in the coldest places on Earth.

In North Alaska, winter temperatures can fall to -62°C. Most Alaskan animals stay warm underground, but red flat bark beetles move around on the icy surface! How do they survive?

FACT >>>
The beetles can survive in temperatures as cold as -100°C.

The beetles lose water from their bodies as temperatures become lower, so they are less likely to freeze.

Anti-freeze in their blood stops their bodies freezing.

Feeling the freeze

North American painted turtles in the northern United States and southern Canada face very cold winters. Temperatures often fall to -12°C. How do baby turtles that hatch in late summer survive the freezing winter months?

Baby painted turtles hibernate in nests underground to avoid the extreme cold.

FACT >>>

Painted turtles can only survive freezing when they first hatch. During other winters they have to find a warmer place to shelter.

When temperatures get very low, the baby turtles freeze. They can survive being frozen for up to six months.

When temperatures rise, the baby turtles thaw out and use their front legs to dig out of their nests.

Dizzy heights

At the top of the highest mountains, temperatures are cold and the weather is rough. There is little oxygen to breathe and few plants to eat. Most animals can't survive in these high places. But Himalayan jumping spiders can live at 6,700 metres above sea level in the Himalayas, the highest mountains in the world!

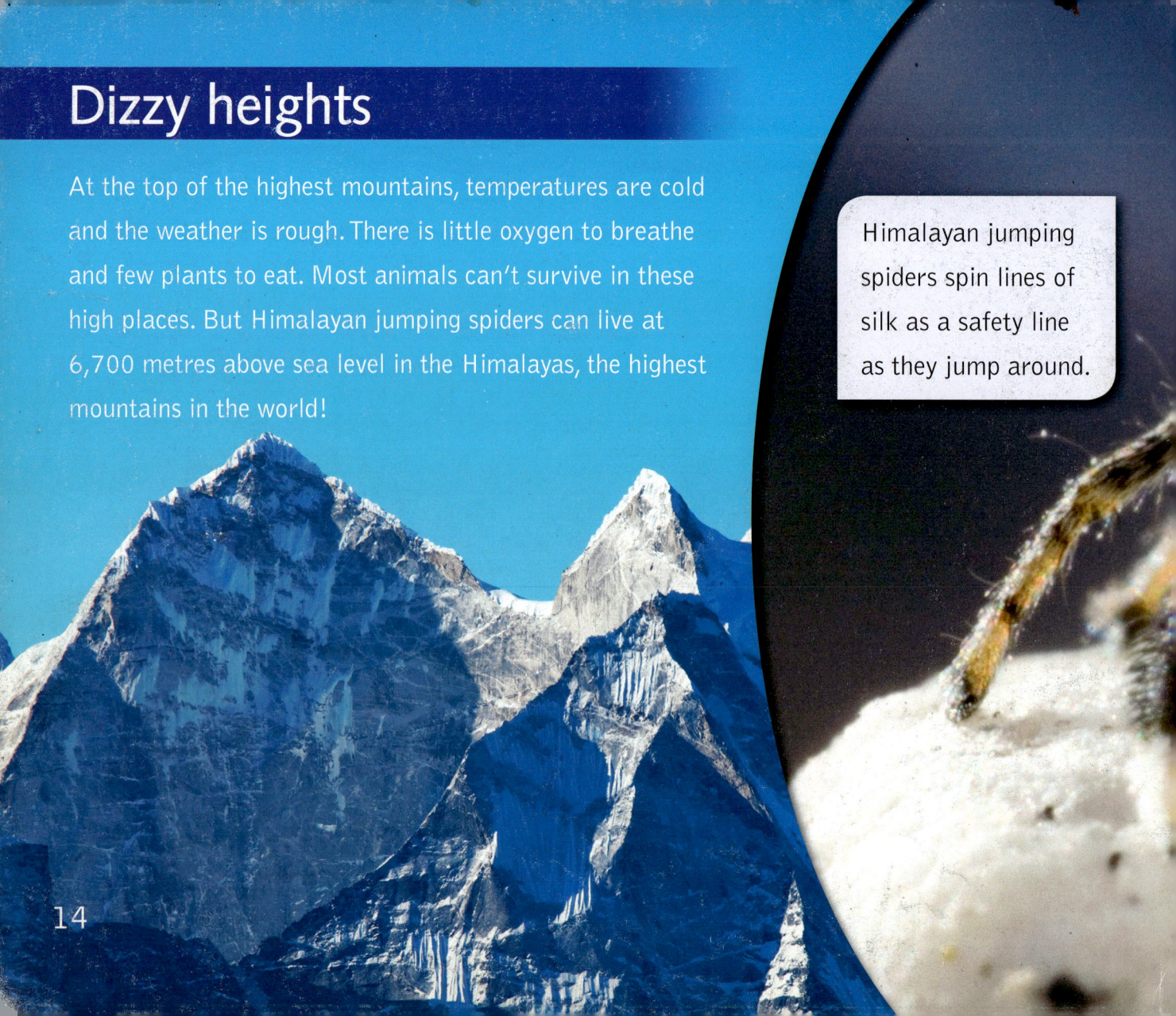

Himalayan jumping spiders spin lines of silk as a safety line as they jump around.

Cusk eels' bodies are mostly liquid so they can survive the pressure of the water.

Long, thin fins on their throats feel for prey.

The eels have mouths low down on their bodies to help them to eat **prey** on the ocean floor.

At the bottom of the ocean

Other unusual animals live in the deepest parts of the ocean.

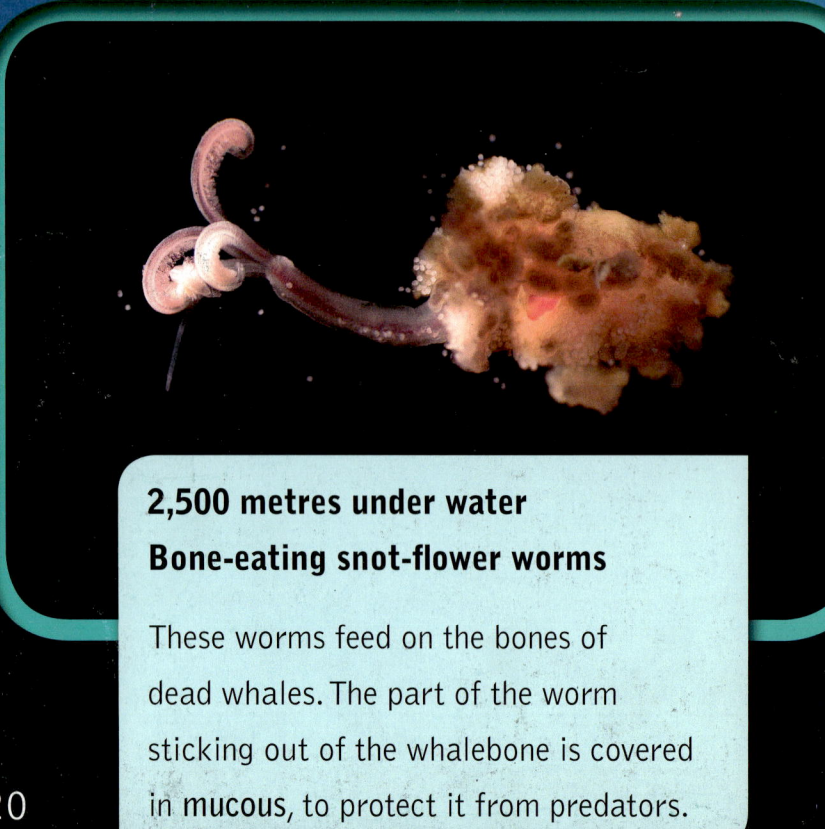

5,600 metres under water
Tripod fish

Tripod fish use their long fins to sit on the ocean floor. They also have fins behind their heads that feel prey moving.

2,500 metres under water
Bone-eating snot-flower worms

These worms feed on the bones of dead whales. The part of the worm sticking out of the whalebone is covered in **mucous**, to protect it from predators.

**7,000 metres under water
Dumbo octopuses**

Dumbo octopuses swim deeper than any other octopuses. The ear-like flaps on their heads help them to hover over the ocean floor looking for food.

Poisonous places

Some of the most extreme places on Earth are poisonous! Even in these toxic places, a few animals survive. Deep under the sea there are holes in the ocean floor called **hydrothermal vents**. They lie over volcanic rock, which heats the water. There are poisonous chemicals in this very hot water. But these vents are home to Pompeii worms.

Pompeii worms have adapted to survive the poisonous chemicals in the hydrothermal vents and water heated to 80°C – nearly as hot as boiling water.

FACT >>>

Pompeii worms are named after the Roman town of Pompeii, which was destroyed by a volcano.

Scientists think the worms can stand the heat and poisonous chemicals because their skin is coated with special **bacteria**.

Extreme defences

Some animals go to extremes to protect themselves from predators. Thorny dragons have adapted to survive in the Australian desert.

Thorny dragons change colour as the temperature rises and the colour of the desert changes. Their **camouflage** makes it hard for predators to spot them.

Pangolins live in Africa and Asia. They have also adapted to stay safe from predators.

Pangolins' bodies are covered in large, tough scales. The scales have sharp tips to put off attackers.

FACT >>>
Pangolins can make a horrible-smelling acid at their rear end that makes other animals run away fast!

The scales overlap so the pangolins can curl into a ball for safety.

Nature's survivors

Many of the world's most amazing animals live in the world's toughest places. They are nature's survivors because their bodies have adapted to the conditions around them.

Flamingoes nest on salt islands in poisonous lakes. They have special beaks that filter their food from the water. They can feed but predators cannot reach them.

The Earth is becoming more extreme, as more places become hotter or colder. Many habitats are flooding or becoming drier. But there will always be living things that can survive when the going gets tough – Earth's extreme animals.

As the planet gets warmer, icecaps in the Arctic are melting. Polar bears will need to adapt to live in this changing habitat.

Glossary

adapted	changed in order to survive better
anti-freeze	a chemical that stops the process of freezing
bacteria	the simplest and smallest forms of life that exist in air, water, soil and living things
blood vessels	tubes for blood to flow through the body
camouflage	the way in which an animal's colour or shape matches its surroundings
drought	a long period of time when there is little or no rain
habitats	places where a particular type of plant or animal normally lives
hydraulic	power from liquid moving under pressure
hydrothermal vents	areas on the sea floor where water heated by underwater volcanoes gushes out
migrate	to move from one part of the world to another according to the season
mucous	thick liquid produced by animals' bodies
predators	animals that eat other animals
pressure	the force with which something presses against something else
prey	animals that are hunted by another animals
soar	to fly smoothly in the air

Index

anti-freeze 11
Asian bar-headed geese 16–17
Australian spadefoot toads 8–9

beaks 26
birds 16–17, 26
bone-eating snot-flower worms 20
burrowing 7

camels 3
camouflage 24
cold 10–13
cusk eels 18–19

Death Valley 6
depth 18–21
deserts 4–5, 8, 24
dry 8–9
Dumbo octopuses 21

flamingos 26
flying 16–17
fringe-toed lizards 6–7

heat 4–7, 22–23
height 14–17
hibernation 12
Himalayan jumping spiders 14–15
hydrothermal vents 22

nests 5, 12–13, 26
North Alaska 10
North American painted turtles 12–13

pangolins 25
poisonous places 22–23, 26
polar bears 2, 27

Pompeii worms 22–23
predators 7, 20, 24–26
prey 19, 20

red flat bark beetles 10–11
running 6

Sahara Desert 4
Saharan silver ants 4–5
scales 25
skin 5, 23, 24
sleeping 8–9

thorny dragons 24
tripod fish 20

water 2, 3, 7–9, 11, 18–23, 26

Adapting to extreme places

Extreme heat

Saharan silver ant

Tough, silvery skin reflects the sunlight.

30

Fringe-toed lizard

Spade-shaped heads help them to burrow under sand to cool down.

Extreme cold

Red flat bark beetle

Anti-freeze in their blood stops their bodies freezing.

North American painted turtle

When temperatures are low, they can survive being frozen for up to six months.

Extreme heights

Himalayan jumping spider

The spiders spin lines of silk as a safety line as they jump around.

Asian bar-headed goose

The geese breathe in and out quickly to get lots of oxygen to their blood.

Extreme depths

Cusk eel

Mouths low down on their bodies help them to eat prey on the ocean floor.

Dumbo octopus

The ear-like flaps on their heads help them to hover over the ocean floor looking for food.

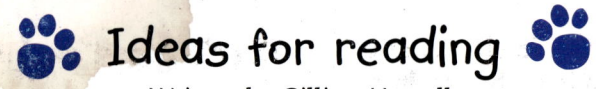

Ideas for reading

Written by Gillian Howell
Primary Literacy Consultant

Learning objectives: *(word reading objectives correspond with White band; all other objectives correspond with Sapphire band)* read aloud books closely matched to their improving phonic knowledge, sounding out unfamiliar words accurately, automatically and without undue hesitation; identifying and discussing themes and conventions in and across a wide range of writing; summarising the main ideas drawn from more than one paragraph, identifying key details that support the main ideas; retrieve, record and present information from non-fiction; explain and discuss their understanding of what they have read, including through formal presentations and debates, maintaining a focus on the topic and using notes where necessary

Curriculum links: Geography

Interest words: poisonous, survivors, temperatures, position, chemicals, oxygen, hydraulic, binoculars, migrate, hydrothermal, Pompeii, camouflage

Word count: 1,500

Resources: pens, paper, whiteboard, internet

Getting started

- Read the title together and look at the front cover. Ask the children what first impression the cover photograph gives. Ask them if anyone has ever seen an animal like this. Ask where they think it might live and why it might be "extreme".

- Encourage the children to suggest what sort of information they might find out by reading this book. Turn to the back cover and ask them to read the blurb.

- Turn to the contents list. Ask the children if they think it will make any difference if they read chapters in sequence or dip in to particular chapters that interest them first. Ask them to choose a section to read first and make notes on it to report back to the others.

Reading and responding

- On p2, point out the word *adapted* in bold print. Ask the children to suggest why it is in bold and remind them to use the glossary when they need to.